I0392563

Surrey Artist of the Year 2014

27 September – 16 November 2014

Organised by New Ashgate Gallery in partnership with Surrey Arts.

The competition is supported by Patricia Baines Trust.
Surrey Life is the official Media Partner of the exhibition.

New Ashgate Gallery
Waggon Yard
Farnham
Surrey GU9 7PS

newashgate.org.uk
Registered charity no. 274326

Editor and design: Samantha Contarini
Cover image: Christine Hopkins, *Blackbeard's Tea Shop*, (2014), mixed media on card.

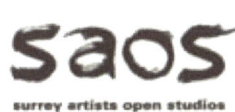
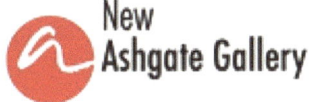
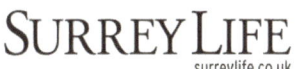

Celebrating the talent in the region

The Surrey Artist of the Year competition gives recognition to the artists who have taken part in the Surrey Open Studios summer event. The prize is in its sixth year and celebrates the partnership between New Ashgate Gallery and Surrey Artists' Open Studios. Each year the exhibition showcases a variety of artwork created in the region.

Votes were counted from Surrey Artists' Open Studios summer event and the artists with the most votes have been invited to showcase their work as part of the Surrey Artist of the Year exhibition at New Ashgate Gallery in Farnham. The public are asked to vote again during the show to choose their three favourite artists. The votes cast by visitors and a panel of judges will decide the Surrey Artist of the Year 2014. The winning artist will be announced at a presentation on 17 October and awarded a solo exhibition at New Ashgate Gallery, as well as a cash prize.

The Surrey Artist of the Year competition is an important part of New Ashgate's mission as an educational charity. New Ashgate Gallery Trust is dedicated to promote and champion the best contemporary art and craft and to provide an unparalleled resource in Farnham, Surrey and beyond. We raise aspirations and inspire excellence. The exhibition enables us to support emerging and established artists in partnership with the Surrey Arts: it coincides with Farnham's Craft Month and we will be offering free public workshops and professional practice seminars to artists. In addition, the exhibition brings new artwork from studios to the market place. It also enables the artists to find new audiences and to develop a relationship with a professional gallery.

I hope that you enjoy the exhibition.

Dr Outi Remes
Gallery Director
New Ashgate Gallery Trust

The importance of arts and open studios in Surrey

Surrey is a county that boasts a diverse mix of urban townships and beautiful rural villages as well as inspiring natural landscapes. It's no wonder then that the county is home to so many talented and creative artists, producing high quality and wide ranging work, from ceramics and calligraphy to printmaking and woodturning.

Surrey Artists' Open Studios is a county-wide membership scheme, offering the public direct access to artists and makers during an annual event in June as well as offering artists a range of other benefits including specialist training and professional development. Open Studios events vary enormously in their scope, with individual artists opening their homes to the public as well as large groups of artists exhibiting together. But they all have one thing in common; they offer an opportunity for the public to see the work being made, to understand the materials and processes involved, and to talk directly with the artist about what inspires them.

In 2000 Surrey Arts, part of Surrey County Council, helped local artists to set up the scheme with these core aims; to celebrate the high quality artwork of local artists, to create networks that offer support and share information, and to increase the contact between artist and the public in order to develop and engage new audiences locally. Today the scheme continues to thrive with over 250 artists participating in Open Studios each year and about 18,000 people visiting Open Studios during two weeks in June.

The scheme continues to promote quality artists and makers and their work; supporting participants to develop their business skills alongside their artwork. As a result the annual event has attracted other Surrey organisations, such as East Surrey College, Guildford Tourism and New Ashgate Gallery, to invest and work in partnership with the scheme to mutual benefit. Each provides a valued partnership that supports and promotes the quality of artwork and the development of artists.

In 2009, the Surrey Artist of the Year competition was set up in partnership with New Ashgate Gallery. This invites the public to vote for their favourite artist during their visits to Open Studios, with the most popular receiving an invitation to exhibit work at the gallery. This helps to raise the profile of local artists as well as providing them with professional development and support to build an audience for their work. Six years on, and the quality of selected artists gets better and better, offering the gallery new artists to promote to their established mailing list and attracting new audience members to the gallery. In turn, it provides Surrey Artists' Open Studios participants with a clear incentive and an association with a high quality contemporary art and craft resource.

In 2011, Surrey Artists' Open Studios announced the move to a membership scheme. An annual membership fee provides artists with their own webpage on a shared website, allowing the public to search for an artist, an online calendar where members can promote their events; a monthly e-bulletin of opportunities and events; access to training and networking events for professional development and of course access to the Open Studios events. There are additional fees to join the Open Studios schemes, but these fees go direct to the marketing of the events. This year we are launching a new website with an online shop, promoting quality art and craft for Christmas.

Surrey Artists' Open Studios scheme was set up in response to an identified need to support local artists and makers. In today's difficult economic climate this is perhaps more necessary than ever, and why the partnership with an established gallery such as New Ashgate is so important, as it enables artists to promote their work and to operate in a competitive market.

Jane McGibbon
SAOS Coordinator
Surrey Arts
www.surreyopenstudios.org

The artists

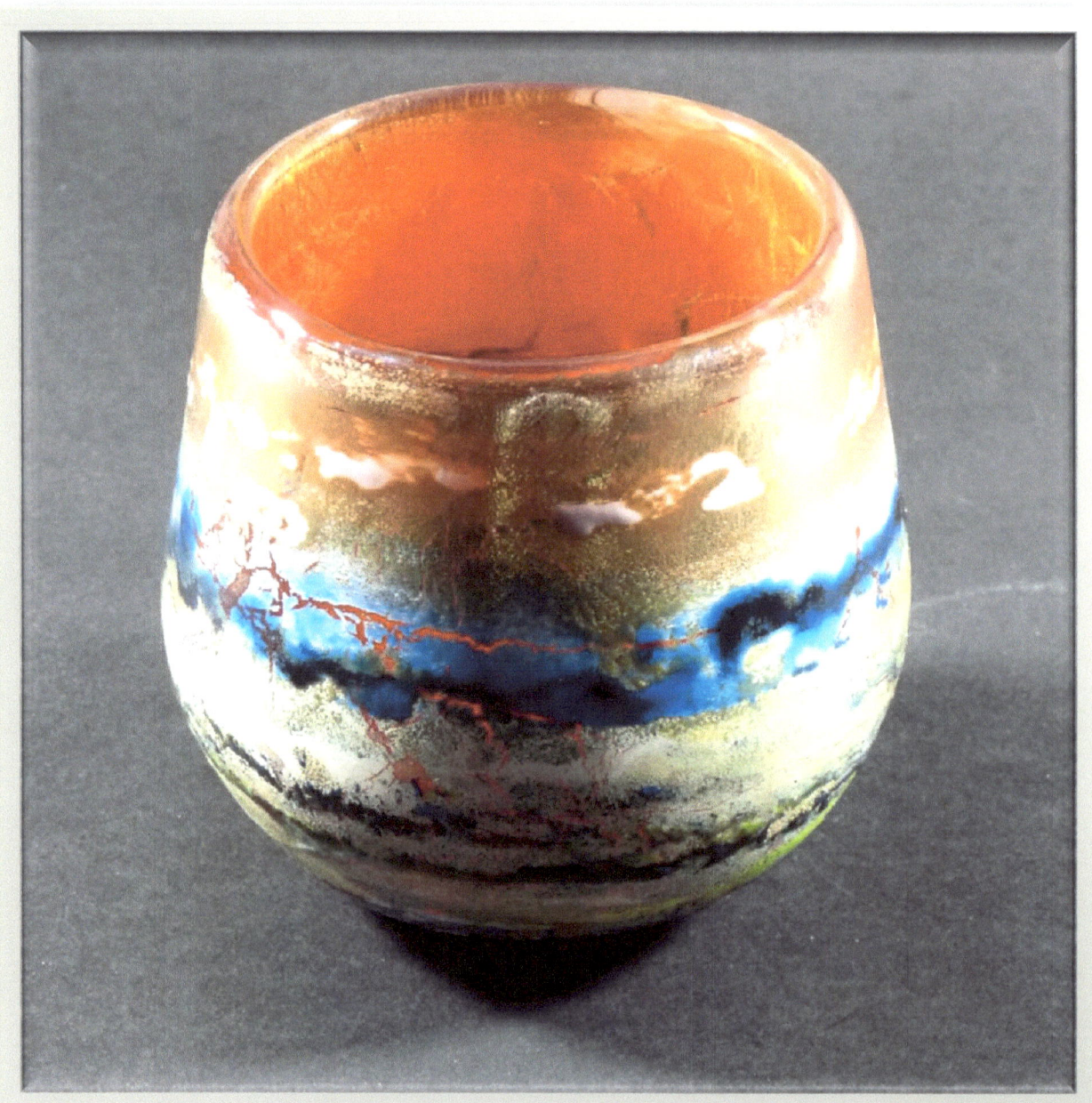

Adam Aaronson

1977 BA (Hons) International Relations, University of Keele

Adam Aaronson has been at the heart of British studio glass for more than 25 years, firstly as a gallerist and subsequently as an artist in his own right, learning glass later in his career and developing self-taught methods.

Adam specialises in free blown glass; his vessels and sculptures are at once a celebration of the simplicity of pure form, and also an investigation into layering. His coloured patinas draw on painterly techniques used by the artists Pollock and Miró, but also inspired by a love of nature and landscape akin to the Impressionists.

Adam's glass work has been exhibited internationally and at prestigious institutions nationally including Kelvingrove Art Gallery, Glasgow and Broadfield House Glass Museum, Stourbridge.

Adam lives and works in West Horsley.

Image: *Summer Sunset,* (2013), glass.

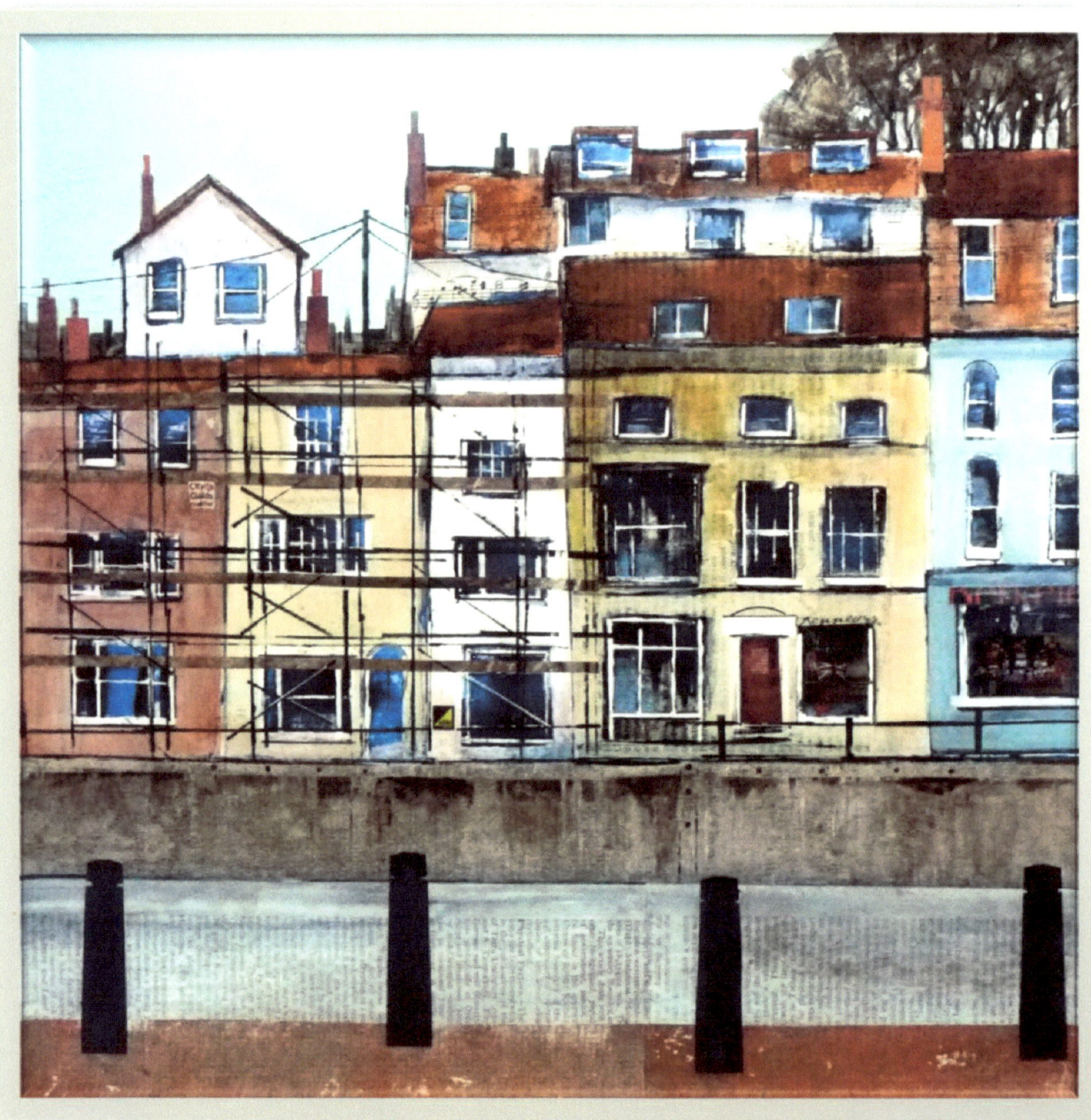

Christine Hopkins

1976 BA Geography, University of Leeds

Christine Hopkins is a painter and printmaker, and is showing mixed media paintings for this exhibition. The use of collage is evident in much of her art, and as well as working with acrylic inks and wax crayons, she uses her printmaking experience to add layers of texture and detail to her finished work. The contents of the recycling bin are often incorporated, although she will often hunt out relevant paper ephemera to use as background to the drawn structural framework which forms the backbone to all of her work. Her love of strong linear form leads often to the addition of scaffolding or other street objects like telephone poles and wiring.

It delights Christine if a viewer recognises the landscape of a painting, as many of them are entirely works of fiction, drawn from careful observation and the memory of many places rather than one specific location.

Christine lives and works in Reigate, Surrey.

Image: *From The Ship Inn,* (2014), mixed media on card.

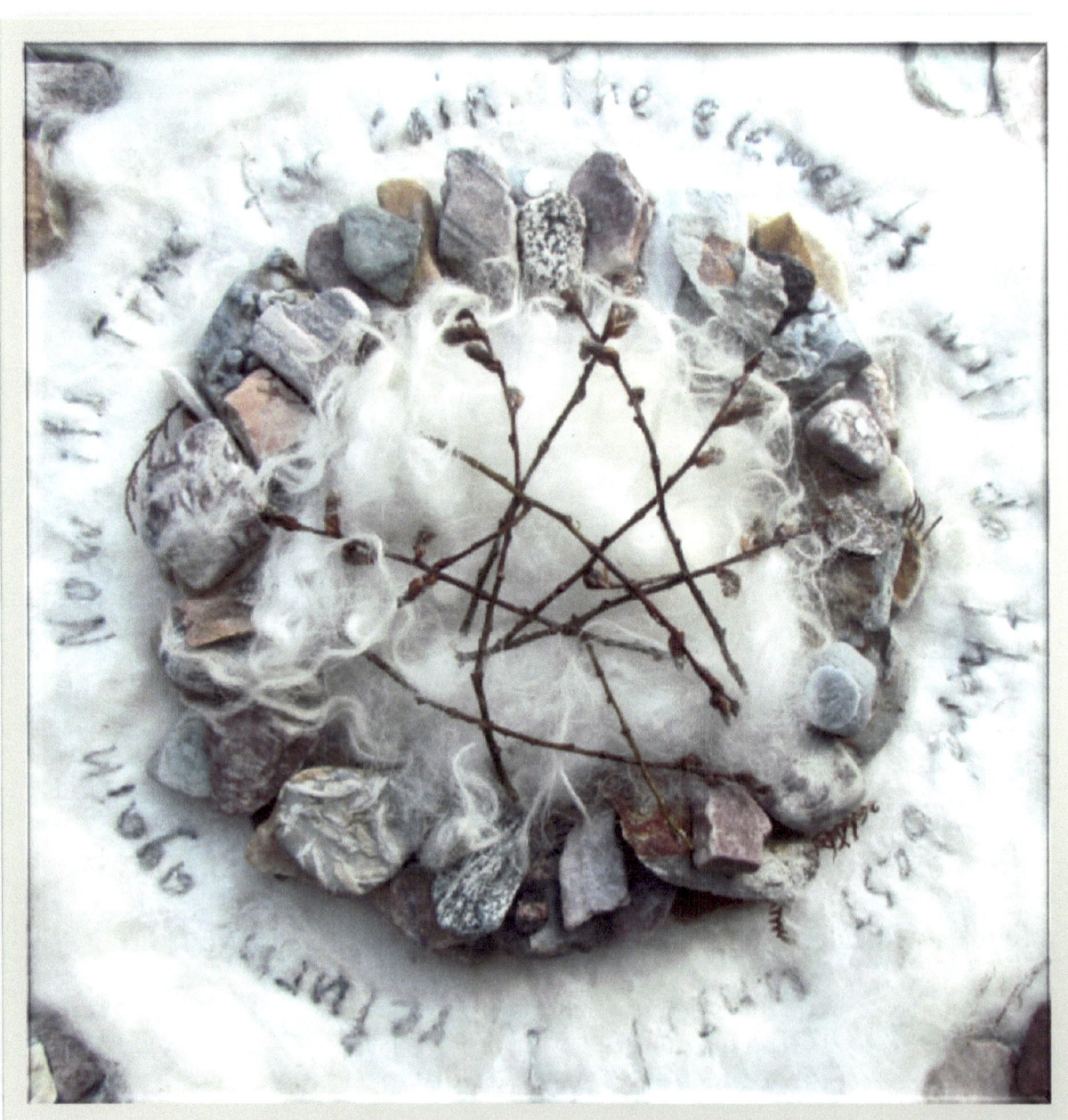

Iona MacKenzie Laycock

1988 BA (Hons) Art and Design, University of Leeds

Inspired by the effect of light on the landscape, Iona MacKenzie Laycock combines wool fibres and hand painted fabrics, creating landscapes based on the Surrey Hills and Scotland.

Earlier this year at her remote family croft on the north coast of Scotland Iona was inspired by a story about couture fabric being buried in the ground to condition it. Following this idea, Iona started to develop new work, placing finished pieces into the landscape to weather over time. This made her focus on raw materials and natural dying processes. Iona built a stone cairn, a patchwork of shapes and colours, placing wool and natural dyeing materials from the surrounding woodland into the centre. From her visual diary Iona was inspired to create the piece *Until I Return Again* (a cross section of the wool dyeing cairn).

Other areas of inspiration are the Surrey Hills where Iona lives, with its wonderfully soft colours over undulating hills, and New Zealand where the landscape has incredible contrasts in colour and texture.

Iona lives and works in East Clandon.

Image: *Until I Return Again,* (2014), wool, found objects and embroidery.

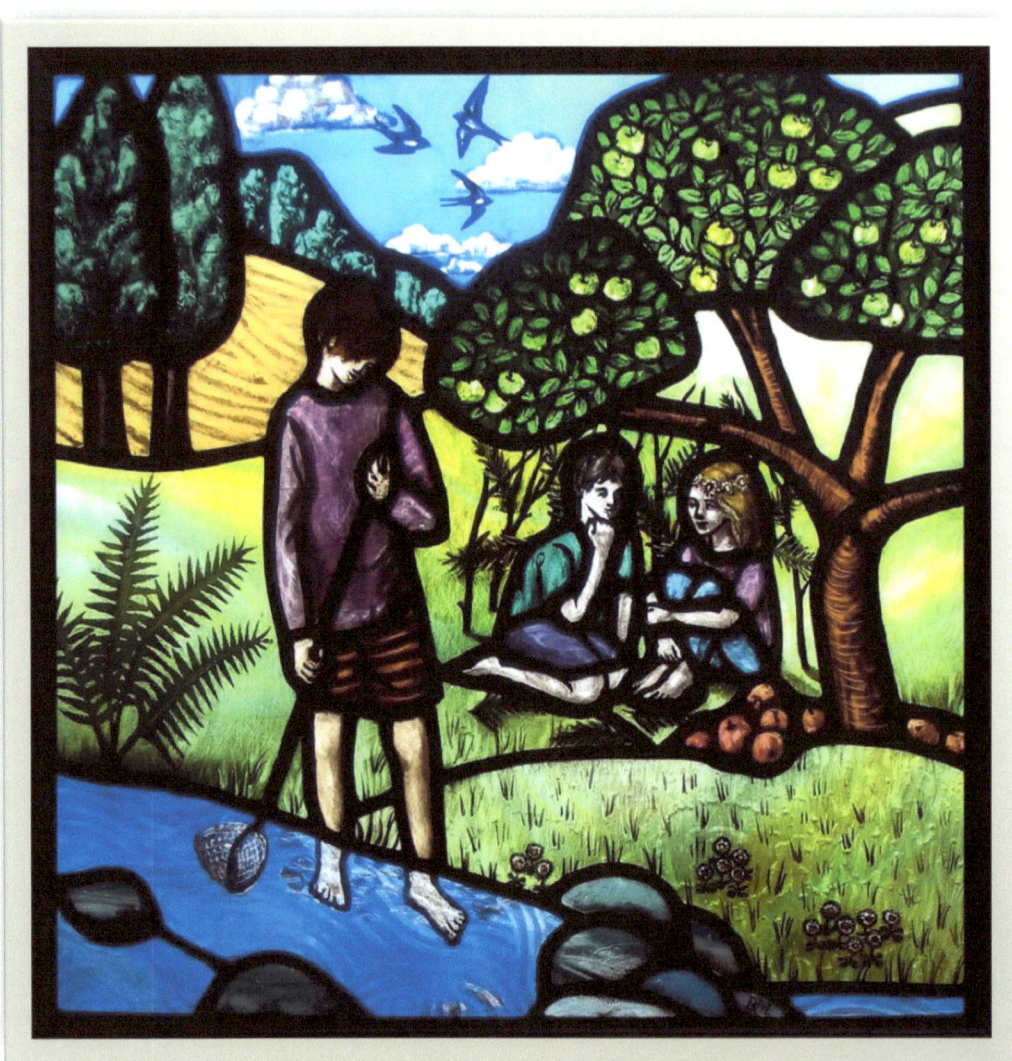

Rachel Mulligan

1995 MA Theory and Practice of Public Art and Design, Chelsea School of Art

1992 Postgraduate Diploma in Stained Glass, Central St Martins

Working in the tradition of the Arts and Crafts movement, Rachel Mulligan is particularly inspired by the windows of Edward Burne-Jones and Christopher Whall. With so many considerations to take into account when creating stained glass – the levels of light, the architectural setting, where the lead lines will go, the choice of glass, how much paint to put on and scrape away to filter the light, Rachel prefers to create all the work herself.

Her other great influence is medieval glass. Before reading was widespread the windows in churches would tell a story and in a similar way, Rachel's work is detailed, descriptive and often has a narrative to it. In memorial panels she celebrates the life and interests of the subject, always drawing on her love of nature and colour.

Most of Rachel's work is made to commission, and she has windows in two schools, The Cassel Hospital in Richmond, Isleworth Town Hall, St Nicholas Church in Cranleigh, and windows in Haslemere Museum and Town Hall.

Rachel Mulligan lives and works in Farncombe.

Image: *Carefree In the Sun That Is Young Once Only,* (2014), stained glass.

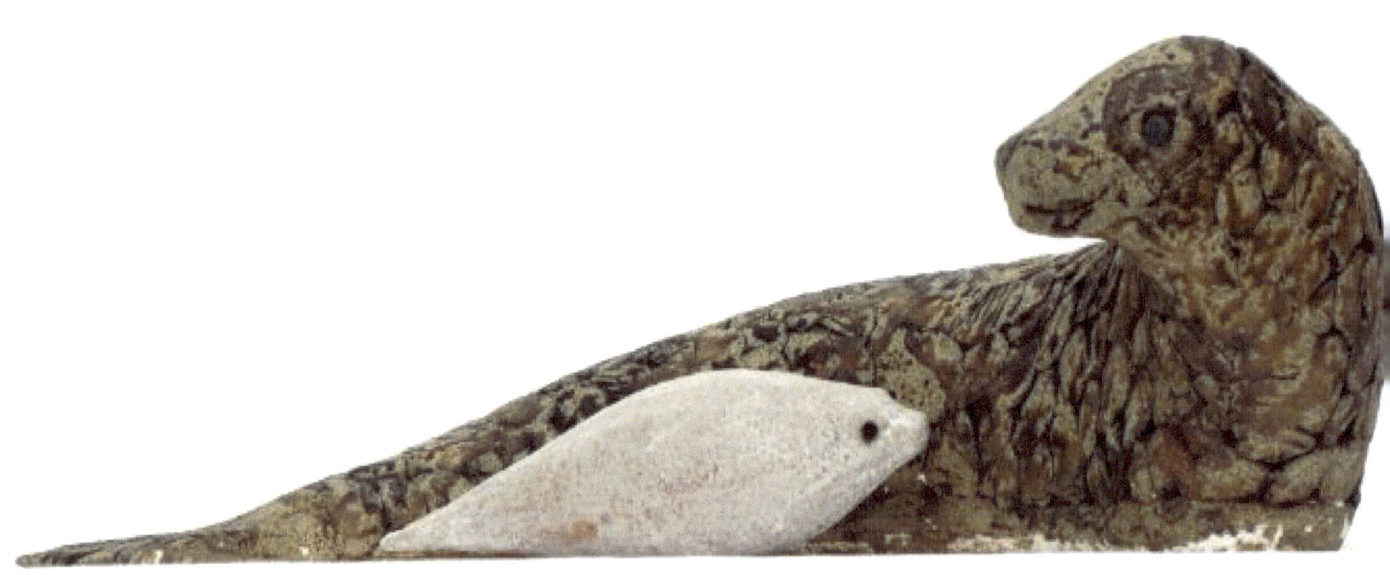

Terri Smart

2002 City and Guilds Certificate in Ceramics, Richmond upon Thames

Terri Smart began creating ceramic objects in 1990 when she was working as an architect in Hong Kong. The feel of the clay and the delight in making a structured piece out of a formless lump became more and more important in Terri's life as she became familiar with the medium.

Terri is influenced by natural elements such as wind and water and she likes to emphasise the contrasts between nature and man, for example in her boat pieces where the size of the boat indicates just how small we are compared to the vastness of the sea. Terri works from her home studio and is constantly inspired by the views over her garden and surrounding fields.

Most of Terri's work is hand-built in textured stoneware clays, and decorated with coloured slips, oxides and glazes before being fired to 1260°C.

Terri lives and works in East Clandon.

Image: *Seal and Pup*, (2012), glazed ceramic.

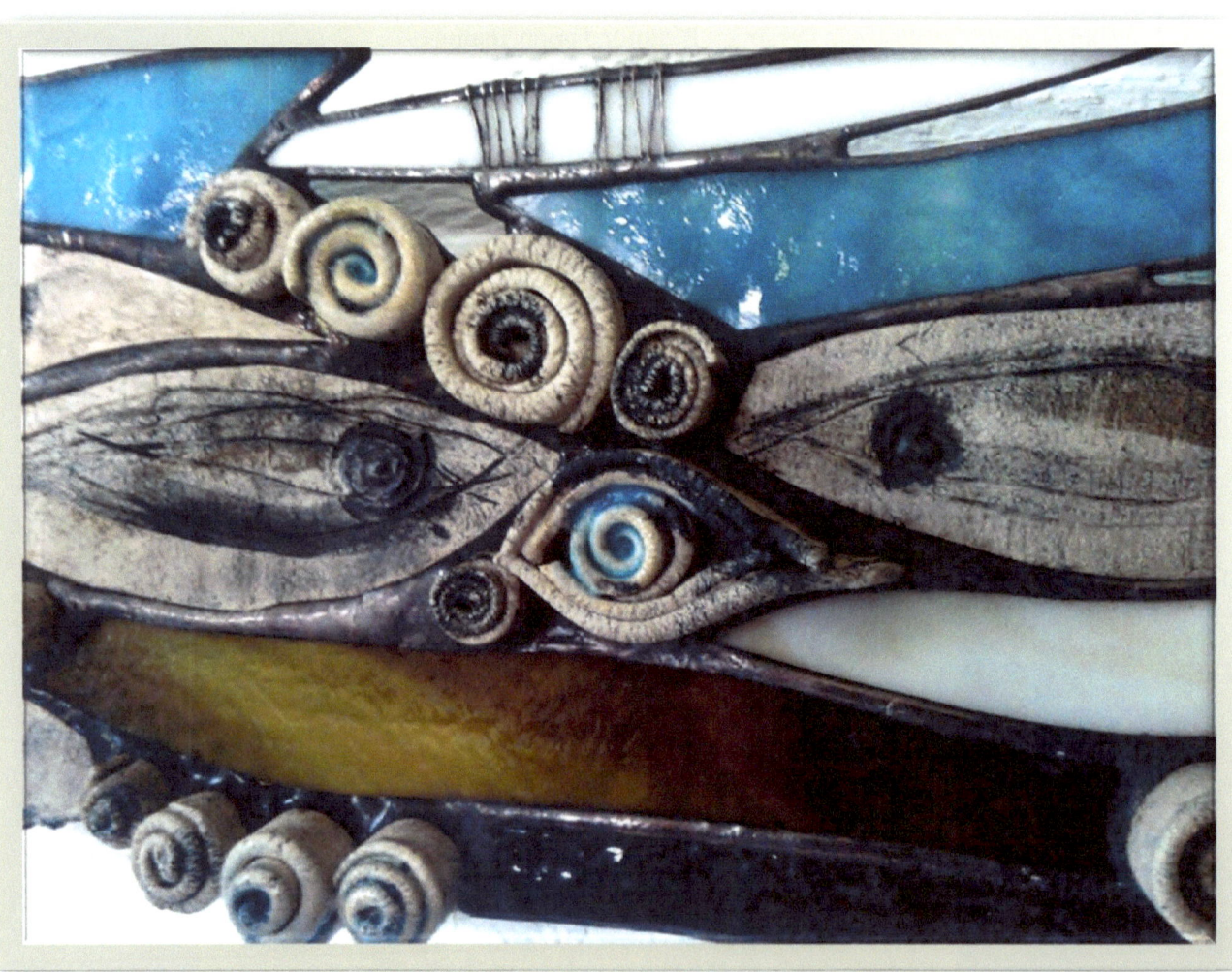

Joe Szabo

2002 Diploma in Glass Painting and Stained Glass Making, Trivium College of Further Education

After training and working as a stained glass maker in his native Hungary, Joe Szabo moved to the UK in 2008 and started to create contemporary glass art in 2D and 3D form. Joe loves sharp contrasts and enjoys stepping away from glass as the primary medium by combining it with other media, such as metal and ceramic. He enjoys experimenting with new ideas and developing technical solutions.

Joe finds eyes particularly fascinating – we always look into someone else's, and, every now and again, into our own eyes. The sea, where the water runs into land is another important source of inspiration for him. He also likes to make pieces that have a historic or art based theme.

Joe works in Buckland, Surrey.

Image: *Odysseus' Adventures – Song of the Syrenes (Detail)*, (2014), glass and ceramic.

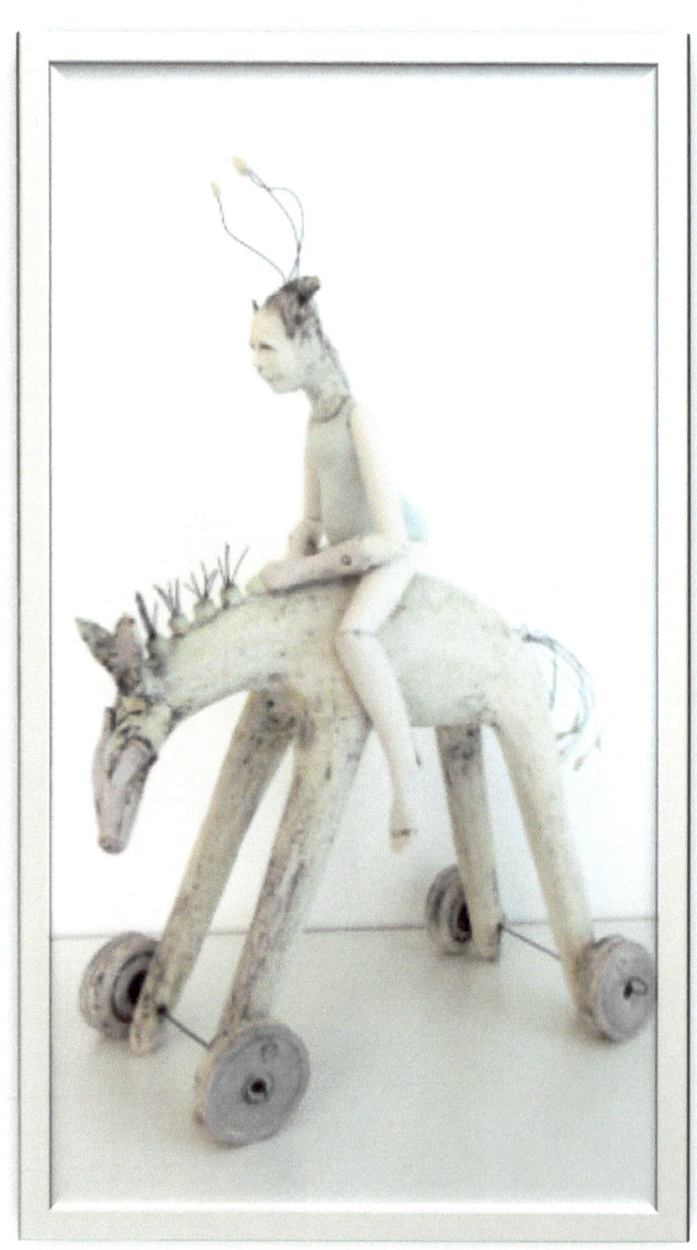

Jean Tolkovsky

1994 BA (Hons) 3D Design Ceramics, West Surrey College of Art and Design

Jean Tolkovsky produces one-off figurative pieces designed to suggest an emotion or small narrative which is often ambiguous and open to interpretation. A visit to the Museum of Childhood in Bethnal Green was the inspiration for her latest works, leading to the creation of doll like figures which reference fairy tales or nursery rhymes, creating in the viewer a sense of nostalgia.

Jean uses stoneware clay which she decorates with underglazes and glazes. Nicrome wire and small metal tacks are also incorporated into the work. All the work is hand built and each piece is unique.

Jean works in Worplesdon.

Image: *She Dreams of Freedom,* (2014), ceramic and nichrome wire.

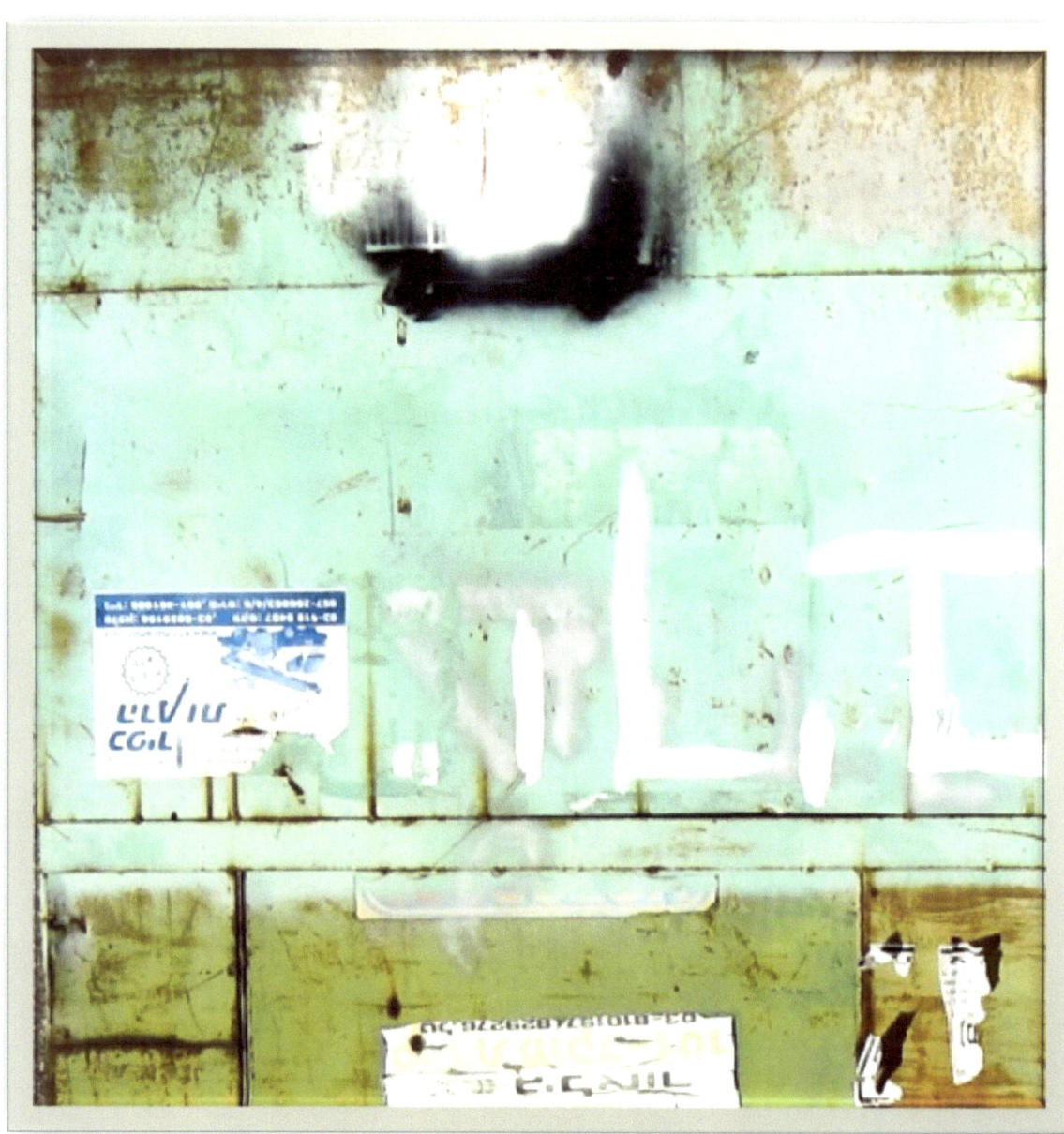

Jim Tucker

1964 HND Graphic Design, Reigate Art School

Jim Tucker's work is concerned with the intrinsic beauty of found materials. Citing the aesthetic of the eroded, weathered and discarded as his main inspiration, Jim aims to blend colour relationship, surface quality, line and form into an art form midway between painting and sculpture. The materials he uses, be they wood, metal, plastic or paper, all have a common denominator in that they all betray the hand of man from a former life.

Jim enjoys the variety of interpretation that found objects afford; there are opportunities to be representational or abstract, whimsical or austere. Recently Jim has turned his attention to monoprinting and photography and painting.

Jim lives in Reigate, Surrey.

Image: *Tel Aviv Green,* (2014), photo on canvas.

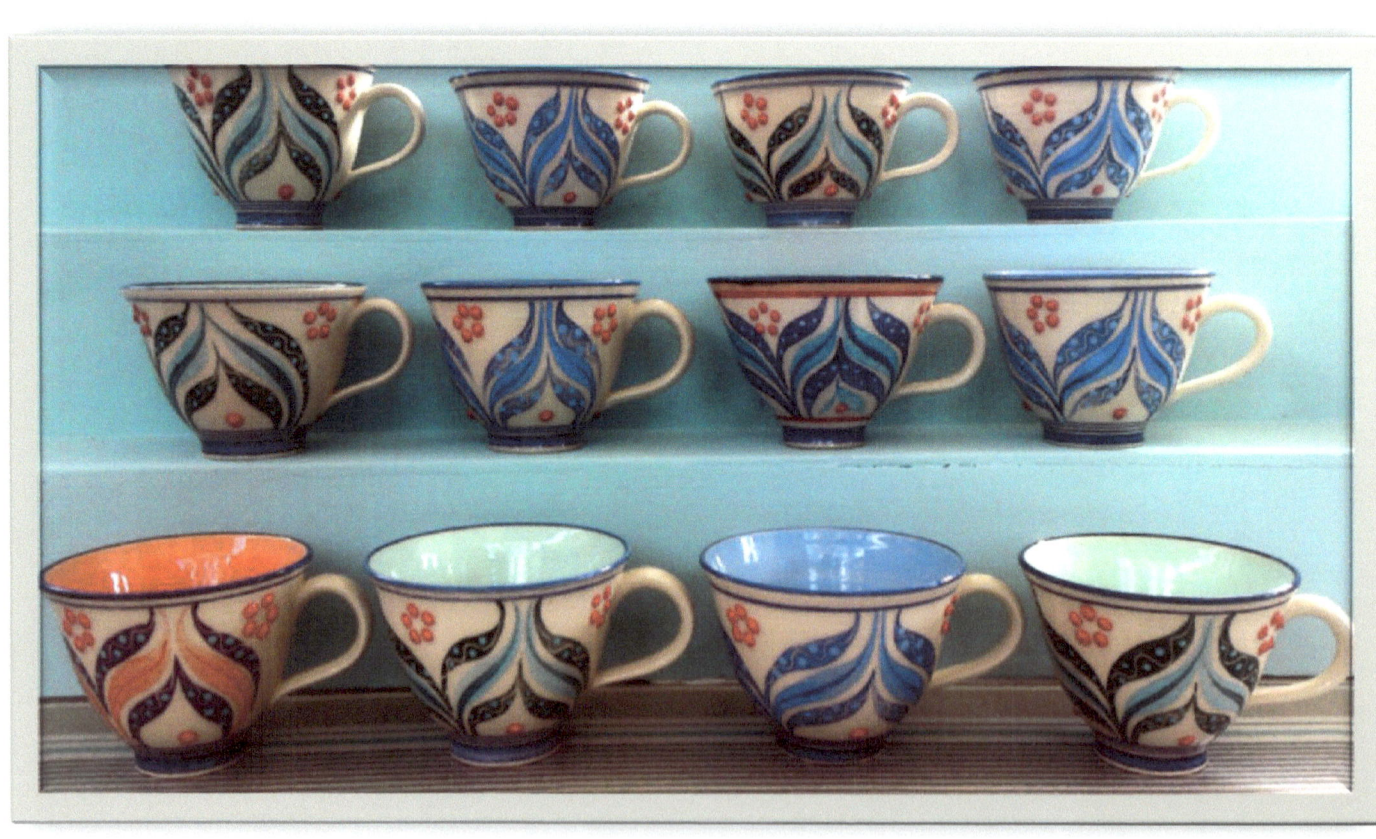

Claire Waterhouse

1989 BA 3D Design Ceramics, Ravensbourne College of Design

Claire Waterhouse is a potter who makes bright and cheerful ceramics for domestic use, thrown on the potter's wheel. Her work is mainly created using white clay and coloured slips, made with a mind to share the pleasure of use, and with particular thought to the presentation of the objects in the kitchen and garden.

Claire creates crisp ergonomic forms which she decorates with vibrant colours in designs inspired by nature and arabesque motifs. She particularly enjoys turning and refining the surface. Sympathetic consideration informs the decoration, and colour combinations are carefully considered.

Claire works in Milford, Surrey.

Image: *Hand Thrown Cups,* (2014), earthenware .

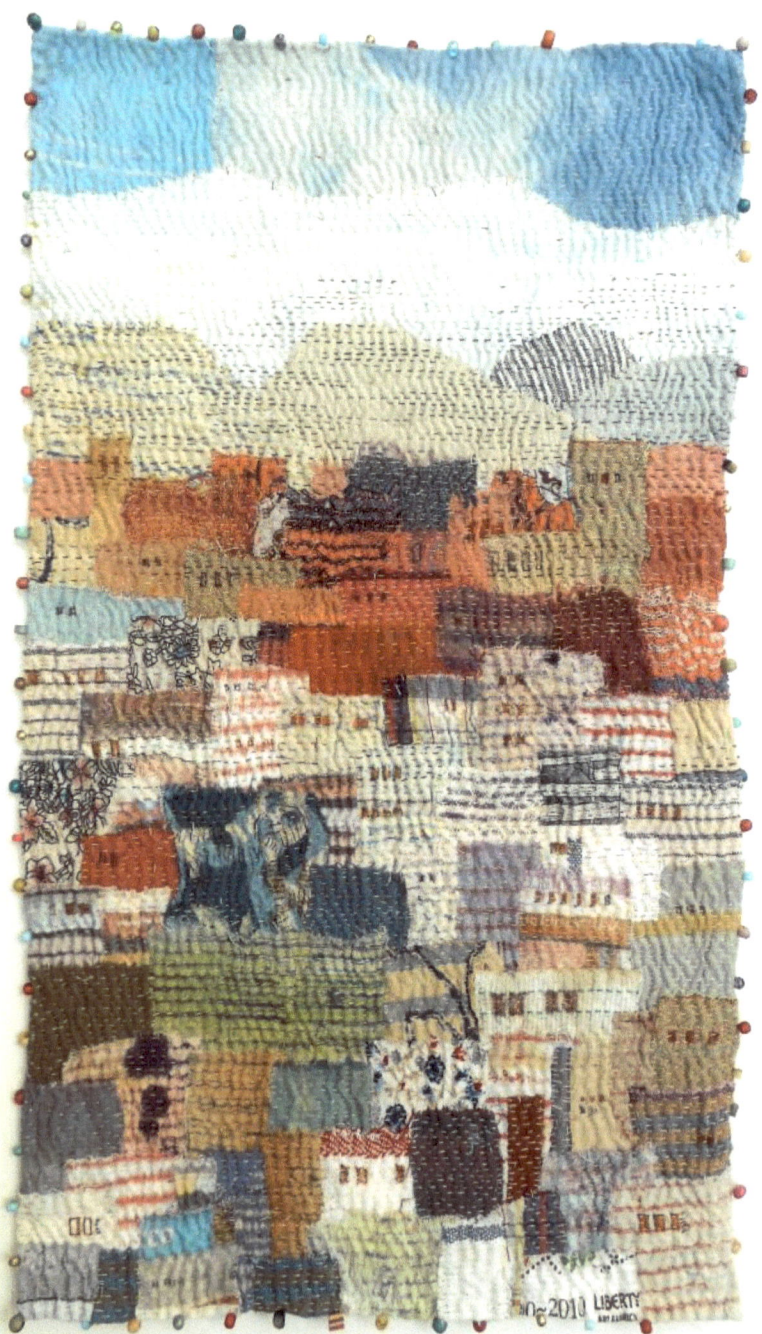

Barbara Westwell

1981 BA (Hons) Architecture, Kingston University

2000 Creative Embroidery Parts 1 and 2, City and Guilds

With a lifelong interest in making and stitching, Barbara Westwell's work has developed into an exciting mix of techniques using photographs printed on to fabric, hand-dyed cottons and recycled clothes, and stitching derived from world textiles.

A workshop in paper collage encouraged Barbara to rediscover her love of old buildings. Her artwork in assembled painted papers completes a creative circle linking her back to her architectural past. In addition, a short tapestry weaving course has added a new skill; Barbara now weaves with fine silk and linen threads and combines the finished pieces with a background of stitching.

Her artwork is now divided between the three disciplines of textiles, weaving and collage, which complement each other in their use of colour, surface texture and attention to detail.

Barbara works in Buckland, Surrey.

Image: *Granada,* (2014), recycled dyed and hand stitched textiles.

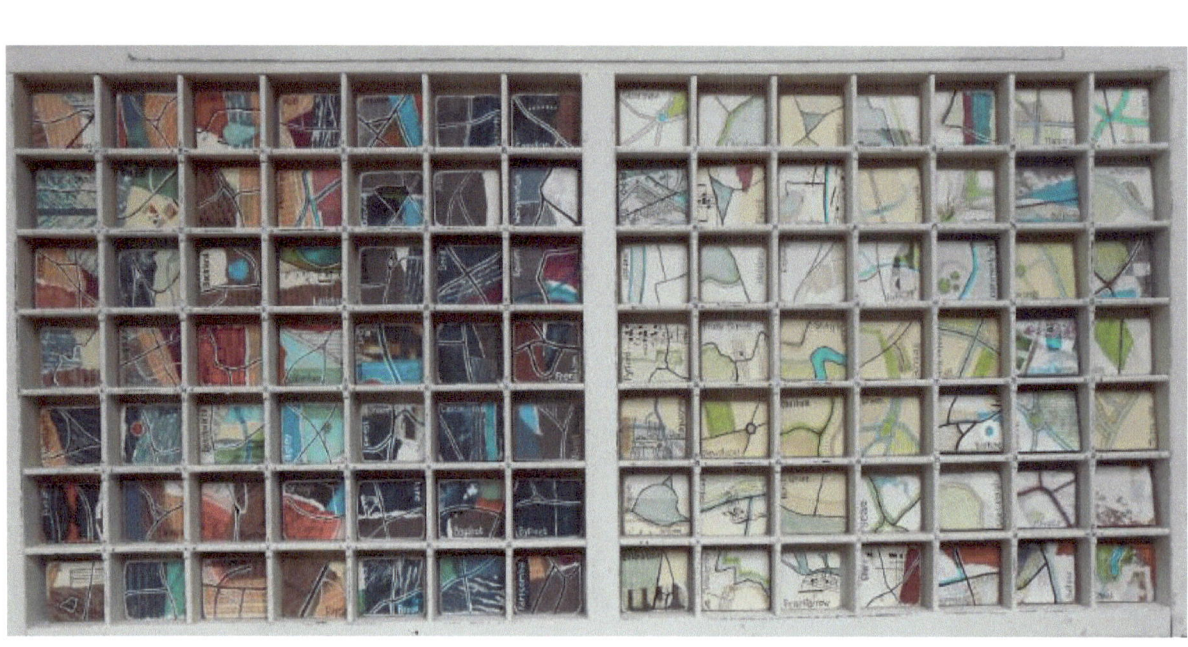

Emily Westwell

2013 BA (Hons) Architecture, Portsmouth University

Emily Westwell uses paint and paper collage techniques to create colourful interpretations of buildings, maps, places and text.

Emily enjoys scouring antiques markets and architectural salvage fairs in search of original and unusual items to incorporate into her work or use as unconventional frames. She also collects ephemera on her travels which are a constant source of inspiration and play a part in her creative process. Emily loves using a broad range of colours and media, and is constantly experimenting with materials to find new and exciting ways of bringing life to her art. She often sands back rough painted surfaces to reveal previously laid colours or the natural texture of the material.

Emily also makes her own rubber stamps to add typographical information to her art. Using this technique she is in demand for creating personalised artwork celebrating holidays, life events and places of personal interest.

Emily lives in Coulsdon, Surrey.

Image: *Exploring Surrey*, (2014), mixed media.

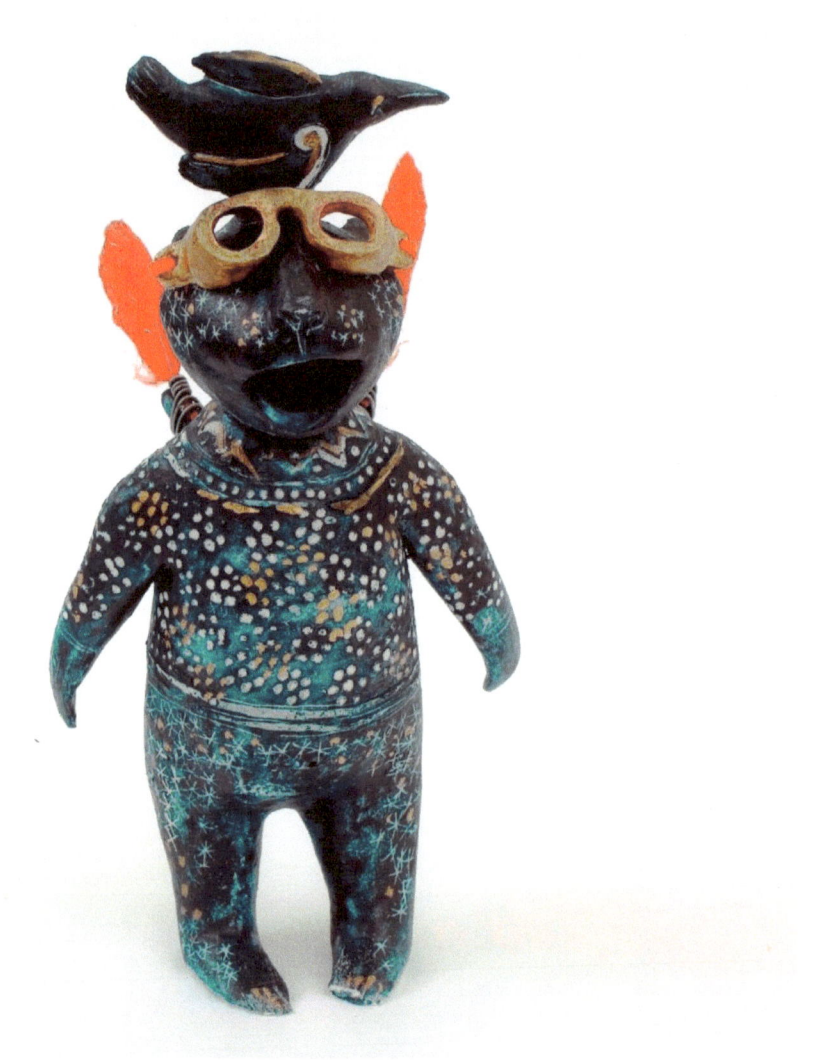

2013 Winner:
Janet Crook

MA Animation, Royal College of Art

Janet has always been interested in movement. She makes small automatons out of found objects, which she then develops into ceramic in an effort to make them last in curious hands. Janet uses simple movements of nodding weighted heads on animals, or wings on fairies from knitted wire. She is still experimenting with other more complicated movements and it keen to see what the next firing will bring.

After studying animation, Janet has had her films shown at the British Film Festival (1987) and at the BAFTA awards in 1986. Janet exhibited her film work at the Tate Gallery and has written music video story boards for bands such as Madness and Dire Straits. Creating ceramic figures seemed like a natural progression from those models she made in her film production years. Janet lives

Janet lives in Dorking, Surrey.

Image: *I believe magic feathers should be stylish*, porcelain.

Notes

www.ingramcontent.com/pod-product-compliance
Lightning Source LLC
Chambersburg PA
CBHW041304180526
45172CB00003B/960